Craft

GW00697371

Before You Start...

The activities are designed for adults and children to do together. With a cupboard or a box full of craft supplies and a spare ten minutes, it's amazing what you can create!

The activities should take about ten minutes once the materials have been assembled. Every child is different and often a project is worth continuing beyond the time limit.

Step-by-step instructions are usually followed by examples showing how to extend the activities. If you don't have the exact materials, use anything suitable you have on hand.

Warning: All steps involving scissors or sharp objects should be performed by adults, not children.

First Activities

Before trying anything more ambitious, help young children practise threading and pasting.

Put some tape around the end of some wool and thread pasta onto it.

Make patterns using beads threaded onto pipe cleaners or string.

Paste things like buttons, pom-poms or fabric onto pieces of paper.

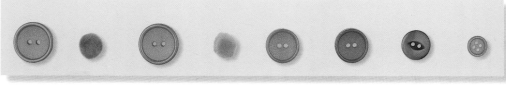

You Will Need...

Make the most of your activity times by keeping a well-stocked craft cupboard.

Essentials

If you only have a few craft materials at home, these are the ones to collect: paintbrushes, paints, colouring pens and pencils, scissors, glue, sticky tape, paper and card.

Luxury Items

Glitter, feathers, pipe cleaners and special types of paper are some of the many supplies that will add magic to your child's craft work.

Things to Collect

Recycle everyday items such as cardboard tubes, egg boxes, buttons and wool for all your craft activities.

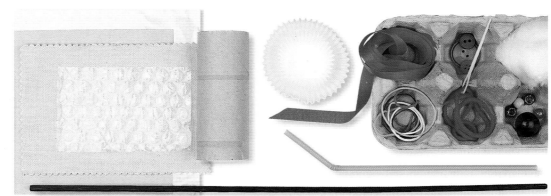

Sewing Shapes

You will need: paper plate, paint, paintbrush, needle, wool and colouring pens.

1 Make twelve holes around the edge of a painted paper plate and twelve more opposite on the inner rim.

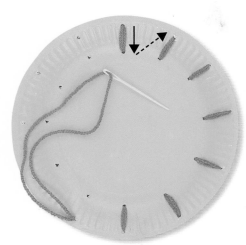

2 Using a kid's needle, begin sewing through the holes as shown.

3 Continue sewing until the sun has all its rays. For older children, number the holes on the back of the plate, especially for more complex sewing patterns.

Give the sun a smiling face using colouring pens

4

Making Skittles

You will need: empty plastic bottles, thick paint, paintbrush, funnel, sand and a ball.

Use several coats of paint if necessary

Add numbers and use them for scoring

1 Soak the labels off six plastic bottles. Fill each bottle with some sand using a funnel. Replace each bottle top.

2 Paint the bottles using thick paint. When they are dry, line them up and try to knock them down with a ball.

Dinosaur Finger Puppets

You will need: felt, scissors, card or craft foam, glue and a button.

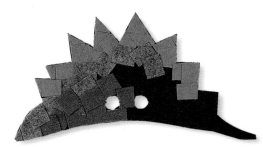

1 Cut out a dinosaur shape from card or foam and make two finger holes.

2 Cut out enough small, square felt shapes to cover the dinosaur.

3 Glue the felt squares onto the dinosaur making sure that the base is covered.

4 Glue on a large button for the eye and add any other decorative details such as the ones shown on the opposite page.

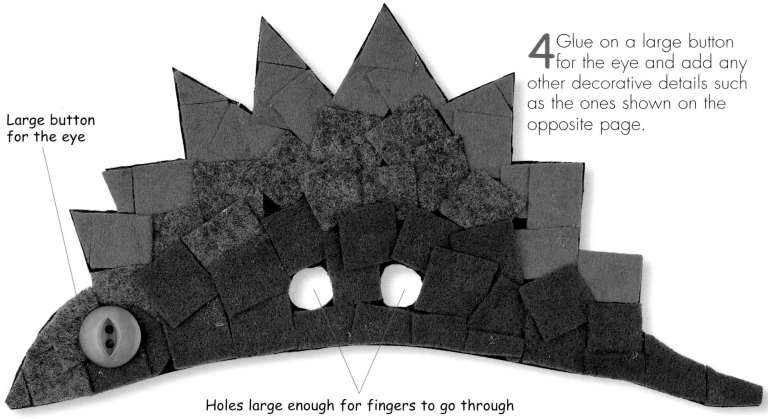

Large button for the eye

Holes large enough for fingers to go through

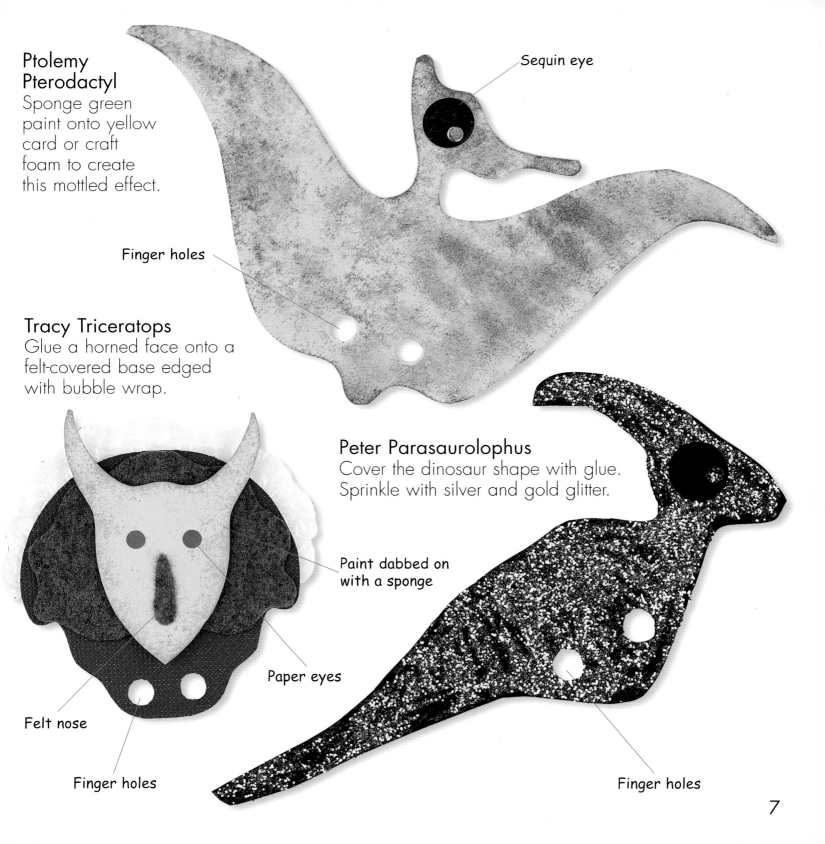

Ptolemy Pterodactyl
Sponge green paint onto yellow card or craft foam to create this mottled effect.

Sequin eye

Finger holes

Tracy Triceratops
Glue a horned face onto a felt-covered base edged with bubble wrap.

Peter Parasaurolophus
Cover the dinosaur shape with glue. Sprinkle with silver and gold glitter.

Paint dabbed on with a sponge

Paper eyes

Felt nose

Finger holes

Finger holes

7

Papier Mâché Plates

You will need: newspaper, plate, petroleum jelly, flour, water, paint, paintbrush and decorations.

1 Tear up some strips of old newspaper. Cover a plate with a thin layer of petroleum jelly.

2 Layer strips of paper over the plate. Brush on a layer of paste made from one cup of flour and two cups of water mixed together. Repeat until there are four layers.

3 When the paper has dried, trim the edges and remove the paper from the plate. Paint and decorate the papier mâché plate.

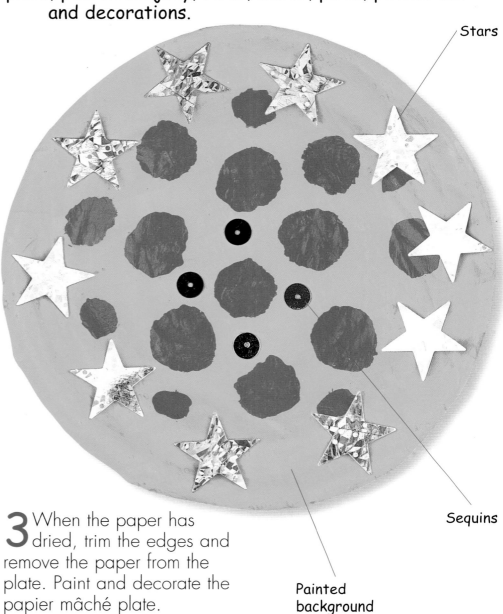

Stars

Sequins

Painted background

8

Face Plates

Use part of the untrimmed paper for hair and then paint on a face.

Fabric flower hair accessories!

Part of a bendy straw

Play Cup

Make some papier mâché using a cup with no handles. Add a layer of varnish or glaze if you have some.

Green painted cup and saucer with yellow spots

Tea Party

Make your own tea set using different sized plates, cups and saucers.

Bright colourful paints make striking designs

Fabulous Frames

You will need: thick card, scissors, glue, fabric, sticky tape and a photograph.

1 Cut out a photo frame from thick card. Be sure the inner dimension is slightly smaller than your photograph.

2 Glue the frame onto the back side of a piece of fabric that is just a little bit larger than the frame.

3 Cut out the fabric at the centre. Make a small cut in each corner. Glue down the edges onto the back.

4 Tape the photograph to the back. Add a piece of string or ribbon to one side if you want to hang the frame.

Choose a fabric that suits your photograph

Jellybeans

Put jellybeans onto a thick card frame using double-sided transparent tape.

Silver foil

Love Hearts

See if you can match the shape of the frame to the sweets or to the photo!

It helps to use sweets you don't like in order to end up with enough for the frames!

Liquorice Allsorts

Big, bold sweets make an effective but simple design.

Thick border for larger sweets

Spooky Spider's Web

You will need: paper, crayon, glue, straws, wool, pom-pom and pipe cleaner.

1 Draw a spider's web onto some black paper using a white crayon.

2 Cut straws to fit on top of the white lines. Glue them into position.

3 Glue two circles of wool to the straws. Finally, make the spider by gluing eight short pipe cleaner legs onto a fluffy pom-pom body.

Place the spider over the wool as though it is weaving its web

12

Fun with Flowers

You will need: jelly or cake cases, paints, paintbrush, beads, straw, scissors, hole punch, fabric and card or craft foam.

1 Find three different sizes of cake or jelly cases. Paint their sides and centres.

2 Cut out two oval leaves from card or craft foam and punch a hole in one end.

3 Use a bead to secure the leaves onto a bendy straw as shown above.

4 Make a hole in the centre of each case. Push them onto the straw and decorate the flower face.

Glitter gel flower face

Use beads or fabric shapes for the centre

Painted pasta eyes

Tie the flowers together with ribbon

Music Makers

You will need: shoe box, scissors, foil, glue, stickers, glitter, cardboard tube, paint, paintbrush, hair elastics, rubber bands and a straw.

1 Cut a hole in the bottom of a shoe box, then cover the box with foil.

2 Decorate the box with glitter, stars, sequins or stickers.

3 Paint a long cardboard tube. Put the hair elastics or rubber bands on as guitar frets.

Plastic straw bridge

4 Glue a straw to the side of the hole, then stretch four rubber bands over the box. Lastly, glue the tube to the box.

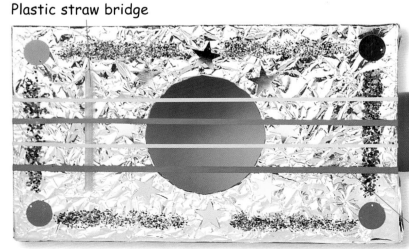

Rubber band strings

Hair elastic frets

Plastic Bottle Shaker

Fill an empty plastic bottle with hard, dried food such as lentils, pasta or rice. Tape strips of paper that rustle to the end, then shake the bottle!

Rustling strips of foil and paper

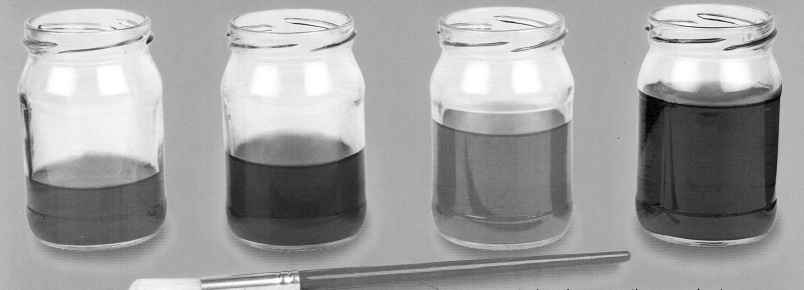

Pasta, rice, barley, lentils or popcorn

Band of card to cover the ends of the paper strips

Jam Jar Xylophone

Fill some jars with different amounts of water and add some food colouring to each one. Test the sounds that the jars make by tapping each jar on its side.

Use a paintbrush or pencil to tap the jars

Sticky Pictures

You will need: paper, scissors, glue, foil, magazines, tissue paper and colouring pens.

1 Cut out a fish shape from coloured card.

2 Glue circles cut from foil and old magazines to both sides of the fish. Put the foil ones at the top and the others at the bottom.

3 Draw in eyes, mouth and gills. Glue strips of tissue paper to the tail. Suspend the fish from the ceiling.

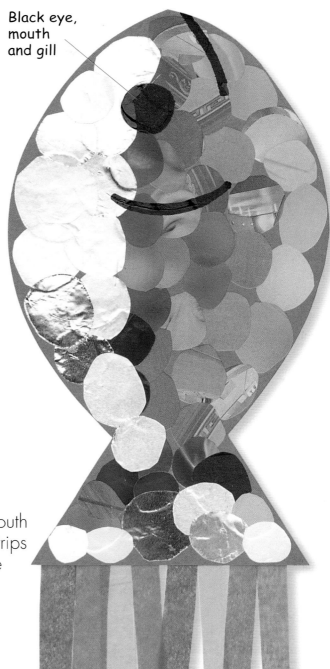

Black eye, mouth and gill

Jolly Jellyfish

Glue tissue paper circles to the jellyfish's body. Then attach long strands of coloured wool for the tentacles.

Long lengths of coloured wool

5, 4, 3, 2, 1...

Cut a rocket ship out of black card. Cover with white paper rectangles. Glue red and yellow paper flames to the bottom, then glue everything onto a large piece of cotton wool.

Black paper rocket shape

White tiles

Cotton wool glued to card

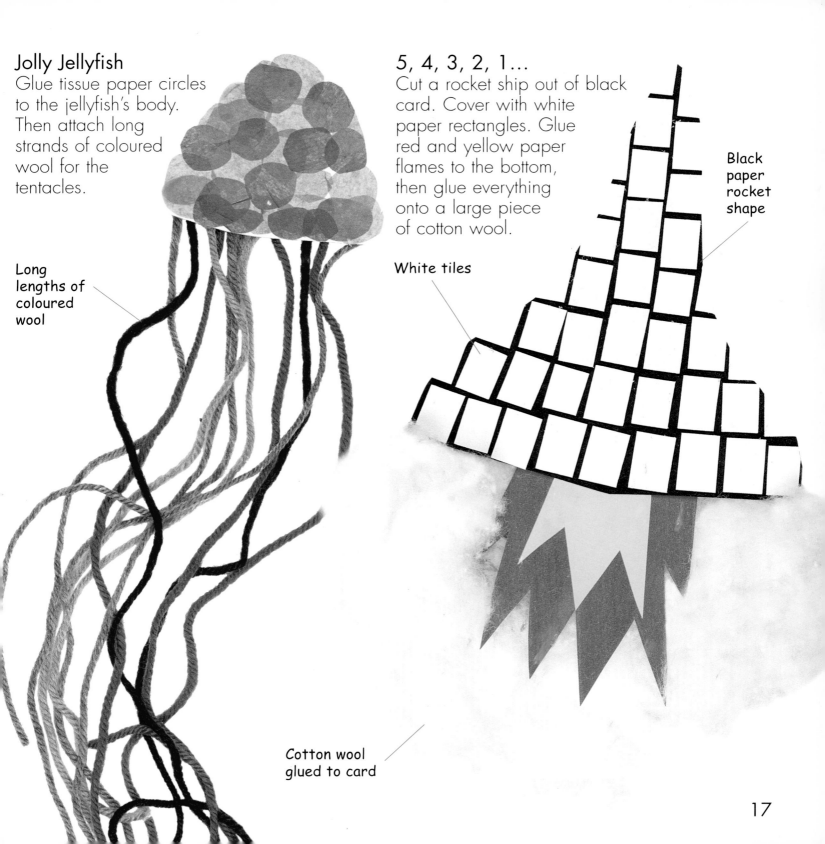

17

Picnic Train

You will need: small cereal box, matchbox, juice carton, paper, scissors, glue, card, foil, paint, paintbrush and a pipe cleaner.

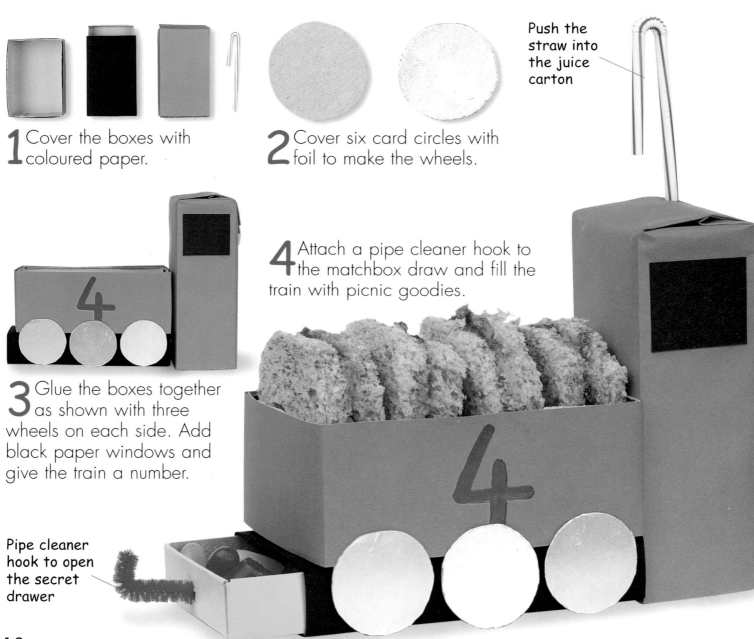

1 Cover the boxes with coloured paper.

2 Cover six card circles with foil to make the wheels.

Push the straw into the juice carton

4 Attach a pipe cleaner hook to the matchbox draw and fill the train with picnic goodies.

3 Glue the boxes together as shown with three wheels on each side. Add black paper windows and give the train a number.

Pipe cleaner hook to open the secret drawer

Container Ship

You will need: cereal box, scissors, stapler, paper, cardboard tubes, paint and glue.

1 Cut out this shape using the bottom and two sides of a cereal box. Then cover it with blue and white paper.

Colouring pens

Paintbrushes and scissors

Crayons

2 Bring the two sides of the ship shape together and staple them at the top.

3 Paint one tube red, one yellow and cover the last one with silver paper.

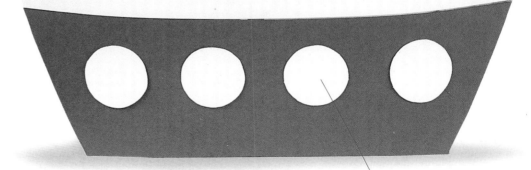

4 Slip the tubes inside the ship and glue on four paper port holes to each side. Use the tubes to store pens, pencils and brushes.

White paper port holes

19

Bat Mask

You will need: egg box, paint, paintbrush, scissors, felt, stick, card and glue.

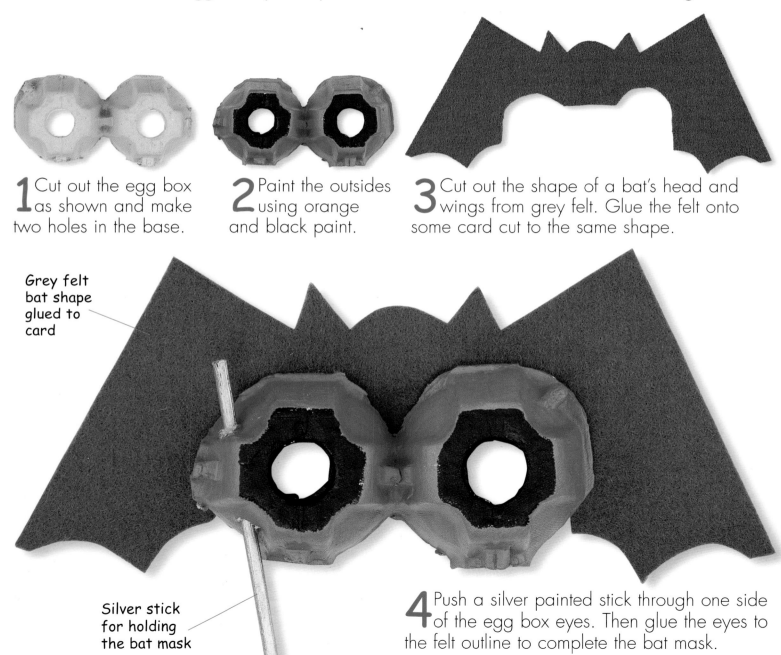

1 Cut out the egg box as shown and make two holes in the base.

2 Paint the outsides using orange and black paint.

3 Cut out the shape of a bat's head and wings from grey felt. Glue the felt onto some card cut to the same shape.

Grey felt
bat shape
glued to
card

Silver stick
for holding
the bat mask

4 Push a silver painted stick through one side of the egg box eyes. Then glue the eyes to the felt outline to complete the bat mask.

Crazy Caterpillar

You will need: long egg box, paint, paintbrush, pipe cleaners, scissors, card, beads, cotton wool, cress seeds and water.

1 Cut an egg box in half lengthways. Trim the sides to make them even. Paint the carton orange.

2 Glue on pipe cleaner legs. Fill the egg spaces with cotton wool. Sprinkle seeds onto the cotton wool, water gently and cover with paper until they sprout.

3 Make a face for the caterpillar and glue it to the body. The seeds should take about a week to grow. Keep the cress well watered.

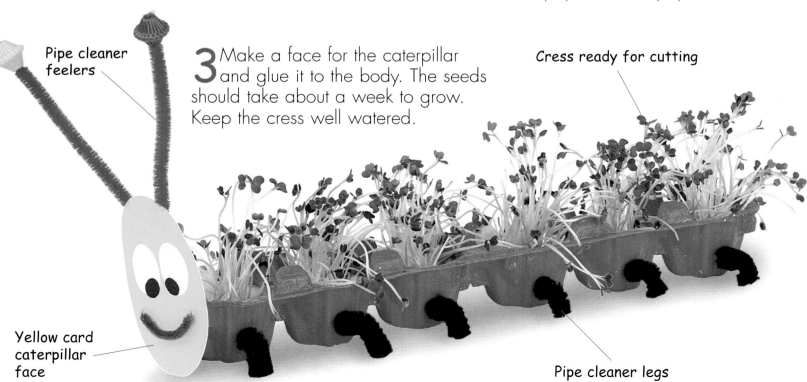

Pipe cleaner feelers

Cress ready for cutting

Yellow card caterpillar face

Pipe cleaner legs

Hats and Masks

You will need: card, tape, glue, glitter, stickers, tissue paper, stapler, felt, pom-pom, stick, scissors, foil, fabric and feathers.

Princess Hat

1 Roll some card into a cone. Tape the sides together.

2 Decorate the cone with glitter and make a border out of coloured stickers.

3 Tape some tissue or crêpe paper to the top and then glue on a sparkly pom-pom.

Yankee Doodle Hat

1 Make a tube shape using some card. Cut the top of the tube at an angle.

2 Cut out a felt circle that will fit around the base of the card hat.

3 Staple the felt to the tube. Push a feather in the hat and call it macaroni!

Love Heart Mask

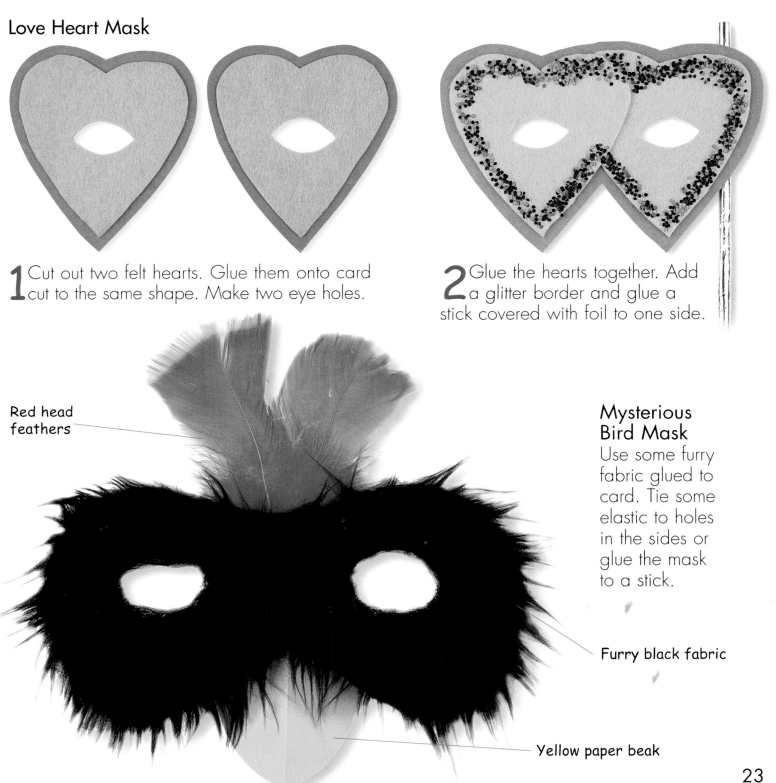

1 Cut out two felt hearts. Glue them onto card cut to the same shape. Make two eye holes.

2 Glue the hearts together. Add a glitter border and glue a stick covered with foil to one side.

Red head feathers

Mysterious Bird Mask

Use some furry fabric glued to card. Tie some elastic to holes in the sides or glue the mask to a stick.

Furry black fabric

Yellow paper beak

Kids' Gallery

With thanks to all the children who helped us make this book.

Super Rocket
by Harry

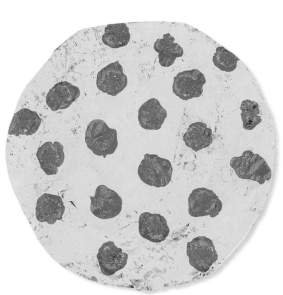

Fairy Plate by Kelly

Sweetie Frame by Oliver

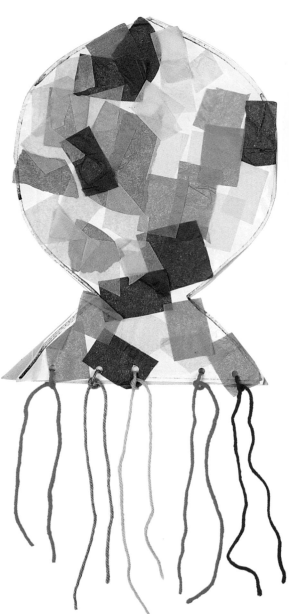

Flying Fish by Natasha